Kids L♥ve Jewish Holiday Crafts

by Tracey Agranoff

Photography by Geoffrey Marshall & Mike Horton

Models: Frumi, Avi, and Malki Mazo
Yosef, Todahya, and Tanya Peterseil

D1121513

PITSPOPANY

NEW YORK ◆ JERUSALEM

Published by Pitspopany Press
Text Copyright © 2000 by Tracey Agranoff
Photography Copyright © 2000 by Geoffrey Marshall and Mike Horton
Cover Photography by Joel Fishman

Editors: Chana Klein and Tiferet Peterseil

Design: Benjie Herskowitz

PITSPOPANY PRESS books may be purchased for educational or
special sales by contacting:
Marketing Director, Pitspopany Press
40 East 78th Street, Suite 16D
New York, New York 10021
Tel: (800) 232-2931
Fax: (212) 472-6253
E-mail: pop@netvision.net.il Web: www.pitspopany.com

ISBN: 1-930143-06-0

Printed in Hong Kong

Thanks and Acknowledgments

Many thanks to everyone who has worked so hard to make this book possible.

To the Editors, Photographers and Craft Testers: your input and insights have been both educational and immeasurably helpful in getting this book "just right" – Thank You All.

I also want to thank the Clergy, Teaching Staff, Students and Families of The Rabbi Bernard S. Raskas Religious School. It has been and continues to be, a privilege to learn with and spend time with all of you. You've made it very easy for me to be creative, innovative and have a lot of fun too.

Special thanks to my very Good Friend, Mentor, Biggest Supporter, and Boss, Wendy Goodman, who said "These projects are great! You should write these ideas down. They would make a great book" – so I did. I couldn't and wouldn't have done it without you!

Dedication

This book is dedicated to my amazing cheering section; my incredibly proud mother, Marion Cass – all those hours making crafts, painting and drawing in my room really paid off Mom!

Remembering my father, Sidney Cass, who has missed so much, but whose memory means so much to me.

My terrific mother in-law, Betty Agranoff. My equally creative brothers & sister – Anthony, Steven, Pamela, and their families.

To my wonderful, supportive, and ever encouraging husband, Ken – I Love You. Thank you for sharing this dream with me.

Mostly this book is dedicated to my beautiful, amazing, brilliant girls, Samantha & Jessica. You make me feel so lucky and proud every day just because I am your Mommy – I Love You!

Contents

ROSH HASHANAH

ROSH HASHANAH APPLE SACHET

You Will Need:
2 squares of red felt - 8" x 10"
white or red lace - 9" x 12"
green felt - 8" x 10"
apple or scented potpourri
scissors   glue

STEP 1 - Place the 2 squares of red felt one on top of the other and cut out an apple shape.

STEP 2 - Fold one of the felt apples in half. Cut out the center of the apple, leaving about an inch around the edge.

 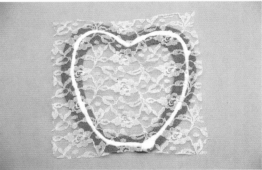

STEP 3 - Apply some glue to the edges of the cutout apple and lay the white or red piece of lace onto it. When this has dried, trim the excess lace from around the edges of the apple cutout.

STEP 4 - Gently crumble the potpourri.

STEP 5 - Place the crumbled potpourri in the center of the solid apple.

STEP 6 - Cut out a leaf shape from the green felt.

STEP 7 - Apply glue heavily to the outer edge of the solid apple and stick the green felt leaf to one of the top corners.

STEP 8 - Trim any excess lace from the cutout apple.

STEP 9 - Place the lace cutout apple on top of the solid apple. Make sure to press the edges together to seal in the potpourri.

Enjoy your Rosh Hashanah apple sachet!

ROSH HASHANAH STAINED GLASS WINDOW

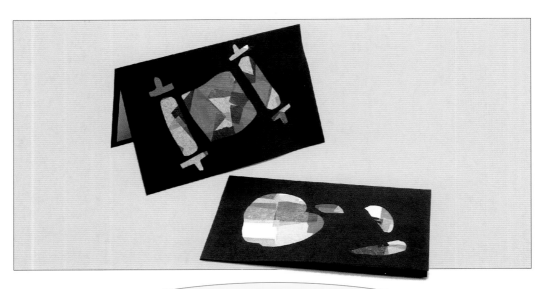

You Will Need:
black construction paper - 8" x 10"
white construction paper - 8" x 10"
colored tissue paper cut into small squares
cotton balls   liquid starch
scissors   glue

STEP 1 - Fold the white construction paper in half.

STEP 2 - Use the cotton balls to spread the liquid starch across the white construction paper. Then place the tissue paper squares on the construction paper.

STEP 3 - Cover the tissue paper with another coat of liquid starch. Set this aside to dry.

STEP 4 - Fold the black construction paper in half.

STEP 5 - Cut out a holiday symbol from the top of the black construction paper. (See Jewish Symbol Patterns pages 137-144)

STEP 6 - Apply glue to the inside of the black construction paper.

STEP 7 - Glue the white construction paper onto the black construction paper. Make sure the tissue mosaic shows through the cutout on the black outer card.

When dried, write your holiday wishes on the inside and share with family and friends!

ROSH HASHANAH MOBILE

You Will Need:

string	crayons or markers	hole puncher
construction paper	scissors	wire hanger

STEP 1 - Cut out 4-6 holiday symbols (See Jewish Symbol Patterns pages 137-144) from the construction paper, each about 3" in size.

STEP 2 - Punch a hole at the top of each symbol.

STEP 3 - Tie strings of different lengths to the cutouts.

STEP 4 - Tie the strings onto the bottom of the wire hanger. Vary the symbols and the string lengths to add interest to your mobile.

Mobiles Are A Fun And Fanciful Way To Decorate For A Special Day. When Placed In Front Of An Open Window The Mobile Pieces Seem To Dance, Telling The Story Of The Holiday.

GREAT IDEA! You can decorate the hanger by wrapping it with crepe paper, yarn, raffia or ribbon.

HONEY BEES

You Will Need:
1 wooden clothes pin   black pipe cleaner
½ sheet of white tissue paper   scissors
black & yellow paint or markers
magnetic tape

STEP 1 - Paint or color alternating black & yellow stripes over one of the flat sides of the clothes pin. Set this aside to dry.

STEP 2 - Insert the black pipe cleaner all the way through the clothes pin opening.

STEP 3 - Gently push 1/2 a sheet of white tissue paper into the black pipe cleaner. The gathering forms the bees' wings.

STEP 4 - Place a strip of self-sticking magnetic tape on the back of the clothes pin.

Place It On Your Fridge Or Other Metal Spot And It Will Remind You That Rosh Hashanah Is Here!

For Some Additional Fun, Add Googly Eyes To Your Bee And Glitter To The Wings!

GREAT IDEA! If you use a hinged clothes pin, reverse the process – tissue first and then the pipe cleaner.

APPLES AND HONEY PLATE

You Will Need:
2 clear plastic plates   scissors
cotton balls   glue   liquid starch
black construction paper - 9" x 12"
1 sheet each of yellow, red and white
tissue paper, cut into small squares

STEP 1 - Cut out 4-6 apple shapes (See Jewish Symbol Patterns pages 137-144) from the black construction paper.

STEP 2 - Use the cotton balls to spread the liquid starch across the clear plastic plate. Then place the tissue paper squares on the clear plastic plate.

STEP 3 - Place the apple cutouts on top of the tissue paper.

STEP 4 - Place glue along the plate rim.

STEP 5 - Take the second clear plate and place it on top of the decorated plate, carefully pressing glued edges together to seal.

Let Dry And Enjoy!

GREAT IDEA! 2 sheets of clear contact paper can be substituted for the plates. When using this method no liquid starch or glue is needed.

ROSH HASHANAH PLACEMATS

You Will Need:
1 sheet black construction paper - 9" x 12"
2 sheets clear contact paper - 12" x 18"
scissors
colored tissue paper cut into small squares

STEP 1 - Cut out holiday symbols (See Jewish Symbol Patterns pages 137-144) from the black construction paper.

STEP 2 - Place one piece of clear contact paper, sticky side up, in front of you.

STEP 3 - Place the colored tissue paper squares and the holiday cutouts onto the clear contact paper.

STEP 4 - Place the second sheet of clear contact paper, sticky side down, on top to seal together.

ROSH HASHANAH BIRTHDAY CROWN

You Will Need:
scissors   stapler   stickers
glue   feathers   tagboard - 4" x 24"
paper scraps   sequins   dried flowers

STEP 1 - Cut a 4" wide strip out of the tagboard. Cut a jagged pattern along the top of it.

STEP 2 - Measure the cardboard strip to fit around your head, and trim away the excess.

STEP 3 - Decorate the crown using feathers, stickers, paper scraps, dried flowers and sequins. Set this aside to dry.

STEP 4 - Staple together and wear.

SWEETIE BEE HONEY HOLDER

You Will Need:
1 sheet yellow craft foam   1 sheet of black craft foam
1 sheet of white craft foam   1 sheet of brown craft foam
empty margarine container with a lid
scissors   glue   pencil
googly eyes   glitter

STEP 1 - Place the margarine lid on the white sheet of craft foam. Trace the lid onto the foam.

STEP 2 - Cut out the circle. Cut the white circle in half and then half again – so you have 4 quarters.

STEP 3 - Repeat STEP 1 using the yellow craft foam instead of white. Cut this out for use in a later step.

STEP 4 - Take 2 of the white foam quarters and glue them to opposite sides of the top of the margarine lid – curved side out.

STEP 5 - Glue the yellow foam circle to the top of the margarine lid (it will cover part of the wings you just glued on).

STEP 6 - Cut out 4 thin strips from the black foam sheet. Glue these onto the yellow foam circle, laying them across like the stripes on a bee – trim the stripes so They fit on the yellow circle.

STEP 7 - Glue on a pair of googly eyes at the top Of your bee. Set the finished lid aside.

STEP 8 - Cut several (6-8) thin strips from the brown foam. Glue these around the bottom part of the margarine container by wrapping them around the container. When the container is covered in this way it will look like a hive for your bee.

GREAT IDEA! Felt can be used in place of craft foam glitter can be added for a shimmering touch.

ROSH HASHANAH APPLE SAUCE CUTOUTS

You Will Need:
colored ribbon or yarn   cooling rack
4½ oz. ground cinnamon   ¾ cup applesauce
holiday cookie cutters or a plastic knife
plastic straw

STEP 1 - Mix applesauce with cinnamon to form a stiff dough.
STEP 2 - Roll the dough to about ¼" thickness.
STEP 3 - Cut holiday shapes (See Jewish Symbol Patterns pages 137-144) out of the dough using the cookie cutters or the plastic knife.
STEP 4 - Use the straw to make a hole at the top of the dough cutout.
STEP 5 - Carefully lay cutouts on a cooling rack to dry. Turn your pieces over occasionally.
STEP 6 - Hang the dough cutouts with decorative yarn or ribbon.

These Smell Great And Make A Very Festive Addition
To Rosh Hashanah Celebrating!

YOM KIPPUR

JONAH & THE WHALE

You Will Need:
yellow index card or construction paper - 3" x 5"
white cutout of a whale (See Jewish Symbol
Patterns pages 137-144)
cut-up pieces of blue and green construction paper
2 sheets of clear contact paper - 8" x 10"

STEP 1 - Draw a picture of Jonah on the yellow construction paper or the index card. The picture needs to be small enough to fit into the whale cutout.

STEP 2 - Trim the picture to make a rounded edge disc with Jonah in the middle.

STEP 3 - Place the disc with Jonah's picture on a piece of clear contact paper, sticky side up.

STEP 4 - Place the white whale cutout on top of Jonah.

STEP 5 - Place the pieces of blue and green paper around the whale to look like water.

STEP 6 - Place the second sheet of clear contact paper, sticky side down, over the picture to seal it.

Now Hold The Picture Up To The Light And
You Can See Jonah Inside The Whale!

SHOFAR 3-D SCULPTURE

You Will Need:
colored tissue paper, cut up - 3" x 3"
tagboard   hole puncher

STEP 1 - Cut out the shape of a Shofar (See Jewish Symbol Patterns pages 137-144) from the tagboard.
STEP 2 - Punch holes all over the Shofar cutout.
STEP 3 - Fold or crinkle the colored tissue paper pieces and insert them into the holes to make a 3-D Shofar sculpture.

GREAT IDEA! Taping down the inserted tissue pieces helps to secure them and makes your sculpture stronger.

SUKKOT

SUKKOT GUESTS

You Will Need:
large roll paper   scissors
crayons or markers

It works best to work in a team for this project.

STEP 1 - One person lies down on a large piece of roll paper. The other person traces his outline using crayons or markers. Then switch.

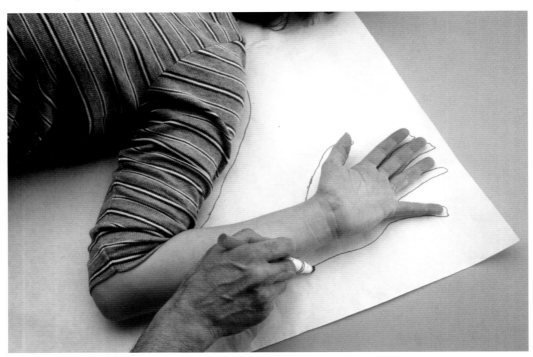

STEP 2 - Use your crayons or markers to color in your guest.
STEP 3 - Cut out your completed guest and hang it on your Sukkah wall.

Make An Entire Party And Enjoy Your Sukkot Celebration!

WIND SOCK

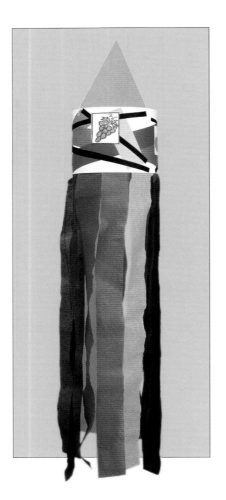

You Will Need:
tagboard - 18" x 4"
markers   hole puncher
string   glue stick
crepe paper streamers
stickers
lick 'n stick tape or shapes
stapler

STEP 1 - Holding the tagboard lengthwise, decorate the tagboard by coloring a holiday design (See Jewish Symbol Patterns pages 137-144) with your markers and using stickers.

STEP 2 - Turn the tagboard over and glue crepe paper streamers along the bottom edge.

STEP 3 - Staple the 2 short ends of the tagboard together to form a circle.

STEP 4 - Punch 2 holes on either side of the circle. Tie a piece of string to each hole and hang from your Sukkah roof or wall.

A Beautiful Sukkot Decoration That Flows With Holiday Wishes!

STUFFED FRUIT

You Will Need:
scissors   string
stapler
1 sheet white construction paper
crayons or markers
newspaper or tissue paper

STEP 1 - Fold the white construction paper in half.

STEP 2 - Draw fruits on the white construction paper.

STEP 3 - Cut the fruits out of the white construction paper.

STEP 4 - Decorate both sides of each cutout fruit.

STEP 5 - Staple the matching pair of fruit together half way around its edge.
Make sure the decorated sides are facing outward.

STEP 6 - Stuff your fruits with crumpled newspaper or tissue paper. Be
careful not to overstuff.

STEP 7 - Staple the rest of the way around until the fruits are closed.

STEP 8 - Staple a string to the top of your fruits and hang.

Perfect For A Sukkot Fruit Salad!

SUKKOT MOBILE

You Will Need:
wire hanger
hole puncher
colored construction paper
string   scissors
crayons or markers

STEP 1 - Draw 6 fruit shapes on colored construction paper.
STEP 2 - Cut out the fruit shapes and decorate both sides.
STEP 3 - Punch a hole at the top of each fruit.
STEP 4 - Tie strings of different lengths to each of your fruit cutouts.
STEP 5 - Tie the other ends of the strings to the bottom of the wire hanger. Alternate string lengths to add interest and to allow the fruit cutouts to move.

Hang Your Mobile From The Top Of Your Sukkah Or On The Wall.

GREAT IDEA! To add additional color, wrap crepe paper all around the wire hanger before tying on strings.

TWIG STARS OF DAVID

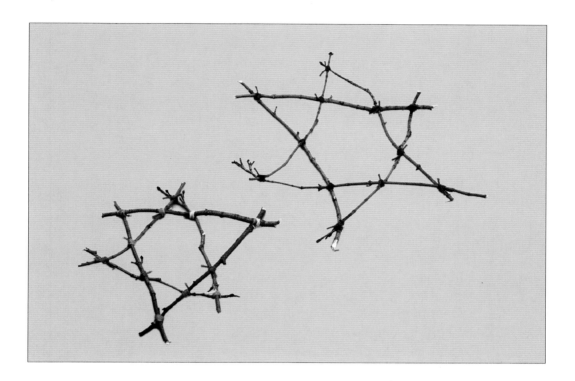

You Will Need:
6 branches or twigs for each star
feathers and beads
glue   yarn

STEP 1 - Tie 3 branches or twigs together tightly with the yarn to form a
triangle.

STEP 2 - Repeat Step 1 with the 3 remaining branches or twigs.

STEP 3 - Tie the triangles together to form a Jewish star. One point of the
star should face up and one point should face down.

STEP 4 - Decorate the star by gluing colored feathers and beads and
by adding a yarn tassel.

STEP 5 - Tie a piece of yarn at the top for hanging.

*GREAT IDEA! Using different lengths of branches or twigs will
create a more abstract star and will be more interesting to look at.*

ETROG AND LULAV

You Will Need:
5 green sheets construction paper - 9" x 12"
1 brown sheet construction paper - 9" x 12"
empty paper towel roll   paintbrush   scissors
empty cardboard egg carton   yellow paint   glue

STEP 1 - To make the Etrog, cut apart 2 egg pockets from the egg carton.

STEP 2 - Glue the 2 egg pockets together, one on top of the other, to form an egg shape.

STEP 3 - Once the glue has dried, paint the Etrog yellow.

STEP 4 - To make the lulav, cover the paper towel roll with glue and roll on the sheet of green construction paper.

STEP 5 - When the glue has dried, cut 3 slits about halfway down the tube.

STEP 6 - To make the lulav branches, cut 5 long strips from the brown construction paper. Two are for the willow branches and three are for the myrtle branches.

STEP 7 - Cut leaf shapes from the second sheet of green construction paper to make the willow and myrtle branches. The willow leaves are long and thin and the myrtle leaves are short and round.

STEP 8 - Glue the green construction paper leaves onto the branches.

STEP 9 - Slide the three myrtle branches on the right side of your lulav and the willow branches on the left side of your lulav. Glue the ends down inside to secure.

POPSICLE STICK SUKKAH

You Will Need:
40 popsicle sticks   glue   scissors
green grass or shredded green construction paper
beads, glitter and sequins   yarn

STEP 1 - Use 4 popsicle sticks to make a square popsicle stick frame.

STEP 2 - Repeat three more times until you have used 16 sticks to make 4 frames. These are your 3 Sukkah walls and your Sukkah roof.

STEP 3 - Glue additional popsicle sticks onto the frames to fill in the 3 walls. Make sure that there is a little space between the sticks so you will be able to see inside the Sukkah from all sides when you are done.

STEP 4 - When your newly created walls are dried, tie 3 walls together at the corners by using your yarn.

STEP 5 - Tie the fourth wall on top of your structure to form the roof. Make sure to secure all 4 corners.

STEP 6 - Glue grass or shredded green paper to the roof of your Sukkah.

STEP 7 - Decorate the Sukkah as you like, using the beads, glitter and sequins.

SUKKOT SUNCATCHER

You Will Need:
colorful leaves   glitter
hole puncher   2 sheets clear contact paper - 8" x 10"
string for hanging   scissors

STEP 1 - Place the leaves and the glitter any way you like on a piece of contact paper, sticky side up.

STEP 2 - Place the second piece of clear contact paper, sticky side down, on top to seal it.

STEP 3 - Punch a hole at the top and hang it where the sun shines for a great glittery display!

GREAT IDEA! Adding additional holes at the bottom or all the way around your suncatcher allows you to decorate with yarn fringes or a fancy stitched frame.

SIMCHAT TORAH

PERSONAL TORAH

You Will Need:
glue   2 empty paper towel rolls
yarn or ribbon black marker
white paper - 6" x 18" (cut a 12" x 18" sheet of paper in half)
2 sheets brown construction paper - 9" x 12"

STEP 1 - Write the word "Beresheet" in the middle of the white paper.

STEP 2 - Apply glue to one sheet of the brown paper. Roll this around one of the paper towel rolls. Repeat this with the other paper towel roll.

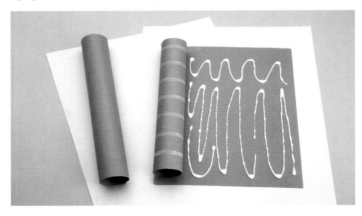

STEP 3 - Place glue 6" from either side of the white paper.

STEP 4 - Place the covered paper towel rolls on top of the glue. Set this aside to dry.

STEP 5 - Roll the paper towel rolls towards the middle at the same time to form a scroll meeting in the center.

STEP 6 - Tie with a ribbon or yarn.

GREAT IDEA! To add additional color, wrap crepe paper all around the wire hanger before tying on strings.

TORAH COSTUME

You Will Need:
2 sheets of white paper -12" x 18"
one sheet of brown construction paper - 12" x 18"
2 strips of construction paper - 3" x 12" glue
crayons, paints or markers
scissors   stapler

STEP 1 - Decorate the 2 sheets of white paper with Jewish symbols (See Jewish Symbol Patterns pages 137-144)

STEP 2 - Cut 8 Torah handles out of the brown construction paper.

STEP 3 - Glue the Torah handles to the back of your decorated white sheets, 2 on the top and 2 on the bottom of each sheet.

STEP 4 - To put the Torah together, staple one strip of paper to the right shoulder of the Torah and one to the left. Repeat on the other side to make a sandwich board Torah.

STEP 5 - Slip the costume over your head, so that you have a strap resting on each of your shoulders.

There You Have It – A Torah That Is Ready To Wear!

TORAH CROWN

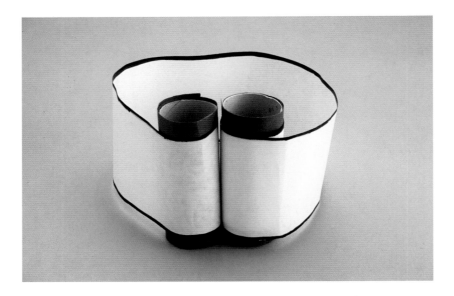

You Will Need:
2 toilet paper rolls   scissors
1 sheet brown construction paper - 9" x 12"
1 sheet white paper - 3" x 36"
black marker   glue or gluestick

STEP 1 - Cut the sheet of brown construction paper in half, lengthwise.

STEP 2 - Cover the 2 pieces of paper with glue and roll them onto the 2 toilet paper rolls, covering them. Set these aside to dry.

STEP 3 - Use the black marker to draw an outline all the way around the edges and on both sides of the long white paper.

STEP 4 - Put some glue on the "short" ends of the white paper strip, place a brown tube on the glue at each end. Set this aside to dry.

STEP 5 - Start to roll the brown tubes toward each other. Stop part way to make sure the ends meet at your forehead. Glue or staple the ends together to form a crown.

Wear Your Torah Crown With Pride!

HANUKKAH

FINGER CANDLES

You Will Need:
8 sheets of colored construction paper - 3" x 5"
1 sheet of red construction paper - 6" x 5"
1 sheet of yellow construction paper - 6" x 5"
scissors   glue

STEP 1 - Wrap each of the 3" x 5" sheets of construction paper, lengthwise, around a corresponding finger to measure for size. Do not wrap any paper around your thumbs.

STEP 2 - Glue the ends to form 8 tubes. Set them aside to dry.

STEP 3 - Wrap the 6" x 5" sheet of red construction paper, widthwise, around both thumbs, and glue the ends together to form a tube. Set this aside to dry.

STEP 4 - Cut out 9 drop-shaped flames the yellow construction

STEP 5 - Glue one flame to the end of each of the 9 tubes.

STEP 6 - When dry, place one candle on each finger and the larger tube over both thumbs.

GREAT IDEA! Add glitter to your flames for a glittery touch!

SUN GLOW DREIDEL

You Will Need:
1 sheet black construction paper - 8" x 10"
colored tissue paper torn into pieces
1 sheet clear contact paper - 8" x 10"
scissors   tape

STEP 1 - Cut out a large dreidel silhouette (See
        Jewish Symbol Patterns pages 137-144)
        from the black construction paper.

STEP 2 - Fold this in half and cut out the middle
        of the dreidel leaving about a 1" rim.

STEP 3 - Place the dreidel cutout on top of the
        clear contact paper, sticky side up.

STEP 4 - Cut the contact paper to the same size as
        your dreidel.

STEP 5 - Place the tissue pieces in the middle of
        the dreidel.

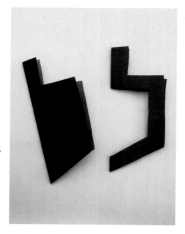

Place In Front Of Window And See The Dancing Colors!

FLOWER POT MENORAH

You Will Need:
10 clay flower pots - 1½" or 2½"   glue gun
wood - 16" x 3½" for 1½" pots   acrylic paints
or   23" x 3½" for 2½" pots   paint brushes
9 metal lock nuts - ³⁄₈"

STEP 1 - Paint the wood any color or pattern you like. Set this aside to dry.

STEP 2 - Turn the 10 flower pots upside down. 8 flower pots are going to be the candles and the last two pots will be the shamash. Decorate the flower pots with the paints. Make sure the pots are completely dry before you move on to the next steps.

STEP 3 - With an adult's help, use the glue gun to glue the 2 pots for the shamash together, stacking them one inside the other.

STEP 4 - Glue the eight pots near each other, onto the wood you have decorated. Glue the shamash either in the middle or on one end of the wood.

STEP 5 - Glue a metal nut onto each candleholder, including the Shamash.

Light Your Menorah
And Enjoy A Fun And Festive Hanukkah!

GREAT IDEA! Instead of gluing them to a board you can set the decorated pots out on a table and have a menorah that can keep changing by how you put them down!

49

HANUKKAH
SHADOW BOX HANGING

You Will Need:
colored tissue paper cut into 1" or 2" pieces   liquid starch
cotton balls   scissors   yarn cut into 6 - 12" strips
2 white foam plates
newspapers   pencil   hole puncher

STEP 1 - Cover your work area with newspapers.

STEP 2 - Turn one of the foam plates upside down. Draw the outline of a Hanukkah symbol (See Jewish Symbol Patterns pages 137-144) in the middle of the upside down plate.

STEP 3 - Carefully cut the symbol out from the plate.

STEP 4 - Use the cotton balls to spread the liquid starch across the inside of the second white foam plate. Then place the tissue paper squares on the white foam plate.

STEP 5 - Put the 2 plates together. The plate with the cutout symbol on top of the plate with the tissue paper, so that the insides of the plates are facing each other (the tissue paper will show through the cutout symbol).

STEP 6 - Punch 5 holes along the bottom of the foam plates and one hole at the top edge of the 2 plates. Tie the yarn pieces to the holes to tie the plates together.

Hang And Enjoy Your 3-D "Stained Glass" Decoration.

3-D DREIDEL

You Will Need:
2 pieces tagboard - 8" x 10"   hole puncher
string   scissors   pencil   magazines
paints   glitter   crayons or markers

STEP 1 - Place both pieces of tagboard on top of each other. Draw the shape of a dreidel (See Jewish Symbol Patterns pages 137-144) on the top piece of tagboard, as large as you can.

STEP 2 - Cut the dreidel shape out of both pieces of tagboard at the same time.

STEP 3 - Decorate all 4 sides of your dreidel shapes any way you like by using the paints, crayons, markers, magazines and glitter.

STEP 4 - Cut a slit in one of the decorated dreidel cutouts, starting at the dreidel point, to about the middle or 4" long.

STEP 5 - Cut another 4" long slit along the second decorated dreidel, this one starting from the handle to the middle.

STEP 6 - Fit the 2 dreidel cutouts into each other using the slits that you have cut. It may take some jiggling to make them fit correctly.

STEP 7 - Punch 2 holes in the handle of one of the dreidel cutouts.

Tie On A String And Hang!

HANUKKAH MAGNETS

You Will Need:
plastic knife or Hanukkah cookie cutters
self-hardening clay or make your own dough (recipe below)
magnetic tape cut into 1" strips   paint

STEP 1 - Roll out your dough/clay to about ¼" thick.

STEP 2 - Cut out various Hanukkah shapes (See Jewish Symbol Patterns pages 137-144) with the cookie cutters or plastic knife.

STEP 3 - If you are using self-hardening clay, then set the dough shapes aside to dry. This may take a few hours to a few days. They need to be completely dry.

STEP 4 - When the clay or dough is dried, paint and decorate the shapes as you like.

STEP 5 - Glue magnetic tape strips to the back of the clay or dough shapes, 1 strip along the top and 1 strip along the bottom.

Put The Magnets On Any Metal Surface.

Easy dough recipe

1½ cups salt
4 cups flour
1½ cups water
1 teaspoon alum

STEP 1 - Mix the dry ingredients together in a bowl, add water slowly, and mix.

STEP 2 - When dough forms a ball around the spoon, kneed well – if crumbly add a little water.

Baking Instructions:
Place the dough shapes on an ungreased baking sheet and bake them in a 300 degree oven until they are hard (about 30-40 minutes).

HANUKKAH
SILHOUETTE PLACEMAT

You Will Need:
2 sheets black consruction paper - 9" x 12"
2 sheets clear contact paper - 12" x 18"   scissors
several strips of assorted colored paper

STEP 1 - Draw several Hanukkah silhouettes, (See Jewish Symbol Patterns pages 137-144) each about 3" high, on the black construction paper.
STEP 2 - Cut out the shapes.
STEP 3 - Place several silhouettes and colored paper strips on the contact paper, sticky side up.
STEP 4 - Place the second piece of clear contact paper, sticky side down, on top to seal together.
STEP 5 - Trim the edges of your placemat so that they look more even.

Use Your Finished Placemat
To Create A Festive Holiday Table!

DREIDEL HANGING

You Will Need:
2 felt squares of different colors
wooden dowel - 10" long
jewel stones   glue   yarn or ribbon
buttons   sequins   scissors

STEP 1 - Glue the top edge of one of the felt squares. Place dowel in this area and fold over, securing the dowel.

STEP 2 - Fold the second piece of felt in half and trace a dreidel silhouette (See Jewish Symbol Patterns pages 137-144)

STEP 3 - Glue the cutout silhouette onto the felt square.

STEP 4 - Decorate as you like using the buttons, sequins and jewel stones.

STEP 5 - Tie yarn or ribbon to both sides of the wooden dowel.

Hang And Enjoy!

HANUKKAH WRAPPING PAPER

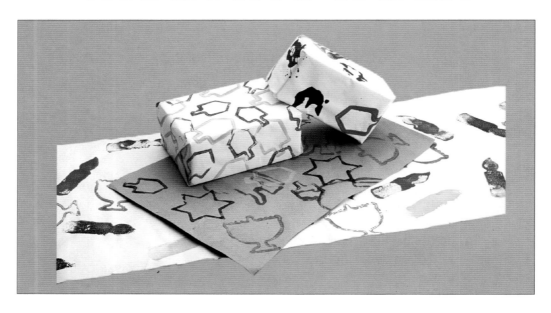

You Will Need:
acrylic or tempra paints
paper plates   white or butcher roll paper
scissors   newspapers   sponges

STEP 1 - Lay down the newspapers to cover your work area.
STEP 2 - Cut Hanukkah shapes (See Jewish Symbol Patterns pages 137-144) from the sponges.
STEP 3 - Dip the shapes into paper plates with some paint poured into them. Use as many shapes and colors as you like.
STEP 4 - Stamp sponge shapes onto the paper.

Now You Have Holiday Gift Wrapping To Make
One-Of-A-Kind Hanukkah Packages!

TU B'SHVAT

PALM TREE

You Will Need:
1 sheet white paper - 12" x 18"
brown washable paint   green washable paint
paint brushes   newspapers

STEP 1 - Lay down newspaper to cover your work area.

STEP 2 - Paint your forearm brown up to the wrist.

STEP 3 - Place you forearm on the paper, elbow along the bottom edge, making a print of your arm on the paper.

STEP 4 - Wash off the arm and paintbrush completely.

STEP 5 - Paint your hand green and place this at the top of your arm print - repeat this several times, these will be the leaves of your tree.

There You Have It: A Tu B'Shvat Palm Tree!!!

TISSUE PAPER TREE SCULPTURE

You Will Need:
4-6 green tissue papers   scissors
4-6 brown tissue papers   glue
white or colored construction paper - 9" x 12"
multi-colored tissue papers

STEP 1 - Cut all tissue papers into 2" squares, roll them up into balls and set these aside. Make sure to keep the colors separate.

STEP 2 - Draw a tree design with your glue onto the construction paper.

STEP 3 - Decorate the trunk of the tree with brown tissue paper balls. Use green tissue paper balls for the leaves, and different colored tissue paper balls for the fruit and flowers.

For older children:

Instead of rolling tissue into balls to make flowers, place the eraser end of a pencil in the middle of a tissue square. Wrap the square around the pencil. Hold the tissue onto the pencil end and dip it in glue. These look like colorful blossoms. Paste them onto your picture.

When completed you will have a
3D sculpture.

63

CRAZY HAIR PLANTERS

You Will Need:
potting soil   scissors
markers or crayons   glue
2 foam or thick paper cups   parsley seeds
3-4 sheets of colored construction paper

STEP 1 - Draw face parts on your colored construction paper. Do not make hair.

STEP 2 - Cut the face parts out. Glue them onto one of the cups to form a face. Set this aside to dry.

STEP 3 - Fill the second cup 3/4 of the way with potting soil. Sprinkle parsley seeds and cover with a little more soil. Pat this gently and water.

STEP 4 - Place the cup of soil into the decorated cup.

STEP 5 - Keep the plant in a sunny spot. Water and wait. It takes about 10 days for the first sprouts to show and then you'll grow a full head of hair in no time.

Holiday Suggestion: Use Your Parsley "Hair"
For Your Passover Seder Plate!

SHLOMO THE TU B'SHVAT SPIDER

You Will Need:
1 skein of black or brown yarn   2 googly eyes
cardboard - 5" x 5"   scissors
4 long black pipe cleaners   glue

STEP 1 - Holding the cardboard in your hand, wrap the yarn around and around the cardboard. Go in the same direction approximately 50 times or more. Make sure the cardboard is thickly wrapped, then cut end of yarn.

STEP 2 - Carefully slide your wrapped yarn off the cardboard.

STEP 3 - Take another piece of yarn and cut it to approximately 10". Tie firmly around the middle of the wrapped yarn.

STEP 4 - Cut open the looped ends.

STEP 5 - Hold the yarn used for tying and hit the spider body against a table to puff it up.

STEP 6 - Insert the 4 pipe cleaners through the body of your spider.

STEP 7 - Bend the pipe cleaners to form the legs.

STEP 8 - Glue on googly eyes.

Welcome Shlomo To Your Tu B'Shvat Celebration!

TU B'SHVAT SEDER PLATE

You Will Need:
2-3 colored tissue papers   liquid starch
dinner-size paper or foam plate   cotton balls
1 sheet white construction paper - 9" x 12"   glue
pictures of seder plate items: *wheat, barley, grapes,*
figs, pomegranates, olives and dates

STEP 1 - Tear tissue paper into strips or pieces.

STEP 2 - Use the cotton balls to spread the liquid starch across the inside of the white plate. Then place the tissue paper squares on the white plate.

STEP 3 - Place the strips of colored tissue over the liquid starch and then apply another layer of liquid starch over the tissue pieces.

STEP 4 - Draw, trace or color pictures of seder plate items on the white construction paper, (See Jewish Symbol Patterns pages 137-144).

STEP 5 - Cut out the pictures and glue them onto the dried tissue paper.

GREAT IDEA! Pictures can be cut out of newspapers or magazines!

FRUITS OF THE TREES MOBILE

You Will Need:
1 sheet brown construction paper - 9" x 6"   string
1 sheet green construction paper - 9" x 12"   scissors
1 piece white tagboard or card stock - 9" x 12"
glue stick   markers or crayons   hole puncher

STEP 1 - Cut out a shape of a tree trunk from the brown construction paper.

STEP 2 - Fold the green construction paper in half, lengthwise.

STEP 3 - Cut a curvy oval shape out of the folded paper to form two tree tops.

STEP 4 - Glue one tree top to the top of your tree trunk. Turn this over and glue the other tree top to the back of the first one.

STEP 5 - Decorate your tree trunk using crayons or markers to draw bark and leaves.

STEP 6 - Punch 3 equally spaced holes in the bottom of the tree trunk. Now set this aside.

STEP 7 - Cut out 3 squares from the white tagboard, approximately 3" x 3". Punch a hole at the top of each square.

STEP 8 - Decorate both sides of these white squares with pictures of fruits and other items that come from trees.

STEP 9 - When completed, tie strings of various lengths to the holes in the white squares. Tie each of these to the holes in the bottom of the tree trunk.

STEP 10 - Add a string to the top of the tree for hanging.

Now Enjoy Your Tu B'Shvat Mobile, Made To Blow
In The Breeze – Just Like The Trees It Came From!!!

PINECONE BIRD FEEDER

You Will Need:
1 large pine cone   plastic knife
peanut butter or vegetable shortening
string   birdseed

STEP 1 - Tie string to the end of the large pinecone making a loop for hanging.

STEP 2 - Spread peanut butter or vegetable shortening thickly over the entire pinecone. Roll covered pinecone in birdseed until the pinecone is completely covered with birdseed.
You can also put the birdseed and the pinecone in a paper bag and shake until the pinecone is covered with birdseed.

Hang In A Place Where You Can Watch And Enjoy Seeing The Hungry Birds Come To Eat !!

PURIM FLIP MASKS

You Will Need:
2 paper plates   glue   tape   scissors
popsicle stick or tongue depressor   stapler
markers or crayons   yarn
2 sheets colored construction paper

STEP 1 - Stack both plates together. Measure and cut eye holes through both plates.

STEP 2 - Separate the plates and lay them upside down.

STEP 3 - Decorate one plate with a happy face and the other with a sad face, using the crayons or markers, colored construction paper and the yarn for hair.

STEP 4 - Turn one of the plates over and tape the popsicle stick to the bottom portion of the plate. Make sure to leave enough of the stick hanging out to hold onto.

STEP 5 - Staple the 2 plates together with the decorated faces facing out.

There You Have It!
A Mask That Can Reflect Your Mood!!

GREAT IDEA! Add sparkle to your masks, decorate with sequins and stickers!

UPPER/LOWER DEMI MASKS

You Will Need:
1 paper plate   scissors   tape
2 popsicle sticks or tongue depressors
markers or crayons   stickers

STEP 1 - Cut the paper plate in half.

STEP 2 - Cut holes for eyes in one of the halves. Decorate this paper plate half by using your crayons or makers. You can make hair, eyes, ears, nose or even a mustache.

STEP 3 - Tape the top half of the popsicle stick to either the right or left side of the inside of the paper plate half.

STEP 4 - Decorate the second paper plate half as if it were the bottom of someones' face. You can make a mouth, chin or a beard.

STEP 5 - Tape the top half of the second popsicle stick to the bottom center of the paper plate.

When Held Up To Your Face
Hardly Anyone Will Know Who You Are!

*GREAT IDEA! Decorate your mask with pieces of
colored construction paper and glitter.*

FINGERTIP PURIM PUPPETS

You Will Need:
crayons or markers   pencil   stapler
1 piece white cardboard - 4" x 6"   glue   scissors
colored construction paper   sequins
yarn   1 empty toilet paper roll

STEP 1 - Make 3 pencil marks along the toilet paper roll, dividing it into 4 equal sections.

STEP 2 - Cut the toilet paper roll along the marks. You should end up with four toilet paper rings.

STEP 3 - Cut 4 oval shapes out of your white cardboard to make your puppet body.

STEP 4 - Staple each oval to a different toilet paper ring.

STEP 5 - Decorate as you like.

Now You're Ready To Begin Your Purim Play.
ACTION!

GREAT IDEA! Pictures can be cut out of newspapers or magazines.

WIGGLE JIGGLE PURIM PUPPET

You Will Need:
several brass head fasteners   glue or tape
popsicle stick or tongue depressor   scissors
colored construction paper   markers or crayons
1 piece white tagboard   hole puncher   yarn

STEP 1 - Cut out the following body parts from the tag board:

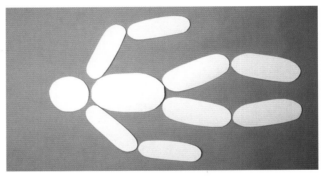

pear shape for the body
circle for the head
4 longish ovals for the arms
4 larger elongated ovals
   for the legs

STEP 2 - Lay your pieces down to see what your puppet will look like.
STEP 3 - Punch holes in the body, where you will attach the head, arms and legs.
STEP 4 - Punch holes in the body parts.
STEP 5 - Insert the brass fastners to connect the body parts. Secure gently.
STEP 6 - Decorate as you like. Use the yarn for hair.
STEP 7 - Glue or tape a popsicle stick or tongue depressor to the back of your puppet body, to use as a handle.

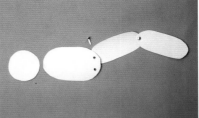

Now Wiggle And Jiggle Away!

SHALACH MANOT BASKET

You Will Need:
3 sheets colored construction paper - 9" x 12"
1 sheet colored tissue paper   scissors
stapler   glue

STEP 1 - Fold one sheet of colored construction paper in half, lengthwise.

STEP 2 - Cut several straight lines from the fold down to about 1" from the edge.

STEP 3 - Cut the other 2 sheets of colored paper into lengthwise strips.

STEP 4 - Open the folded sheet and weave in the colored paper strips. Alternate over and under movements until completely covered. Save at least 1 strip of paper for the basket handle.

STEP 5 - Glue down all the paper strip ends.

STEP 6 - Cut a 2-3" line from each of the 4 corners toward the center of the paper.

STEP 7 - Overlap the cut corners and secure with stapler or glue. Continue this for all 4 corners forming a basket.

STEP 8 - Attach the remaining colored paper strip to 2 opposite sides of the basket to form a handle.

STEP 9 - Place a piece of colored tissue paper inside to line your basket.

PRINCESS HAT

You Will Need:
1 piece tagboard - 12" x 18"
24" long piece of sheer fabric or lace
glitter, sequins and jewels
paint   stapler   scissors   glue

STEP 1 - Cut a semicircle from the long side of the tag board.

STEP 2 - Wrap the ends around to form a cone shape. Overlap and staple to secure. Make sure to leave a small hole at the top.

STEP 3 - Paint a design on the hat. Glue on sequins, glitter and jewels. Set this aside to dry.

STEP 4 - Tie one end of the fabric or lace into a knot.

STEP 5 - Pull the untied end of your fabric or lace through the hole in the top of the cone.

STEP 6 - Secure the hat onto your head using bobby pins, or you can attach string to the sides and tie it on.

There You Have It: A Hat Fit For A Princess!!!

PAPER PLATE GROGGERS

You Will Need:
colored streamers - 4" long
dried beans or rice   1 paper plate
markers, crayons or colored paper
stapler   tape

STEP 1 - Decorate the bottom side of your paper plate with Purim or other
Jewish symbols (See Jewish Symbol Patterns pages 137-144).
STEP 2 - Tape several streamers to the inside edge of the paper plate.
STEP 3 - Fold the plate in half and staple it halfway closed.
STEP 4 - Put some dried beans or rice into the opening of your folded paper
plate. Staple the entire side closed.

PASSOVER

SILHOUETTE SEDER PLATE

You Will Need:

liquid starch   2 clear plastic plates   scissors
cotton balls   1 sheet black construction paper
colored tissue paper cut into 2" squares   glue

STEP 1 - Draw the outlines of the Passover Seder plate items (See Jewish Symbol Patterns pages 137-144) on a piece of black construction paper, about 3" in size.

STEP 2 - Use the cotton balls to spread the liquid starch across the inside of one of the clear plastic plates.

STEP 3 - Lay the tissue squares on top of the liquid starch layer, overlapping as you go, covering the inside of the plate.

STEP 4 - Cover with an additional layer of liquid starch.

STEP 5 - Glue the seder plate silhouettes on top of the tissue paper layer. Arrange them as you like.

STEP 6 - Glue along the outer rim of the plate and cover with the second clear plastic plate.

Your Plate Can Be Used At Your Seder Or
As A Sun-catching Window Hanging.

GREAT IDEA! 2 sheets of clear contact paper can be substituted for the plastic plates.

PASSOVER PLACEMAT

You Will Need:
empty boxes of Passover food   scissors
2 sheets clear contact paper - 12" x 18"
colored construction paper cut into thin strips
labels from Passover canned food

STEP 1 - Cut out box tops, pictures, kosher symbols and recipes from various Passover food packages.

STEP 2 - Place these on the clear contact paper, sticky side up, in any design you would like.

STEP 3 - Add the colored construction paper strips for additional color.

STEP 4 - Cover with the second piece of clear contact paper, sticky side down, to seal the items in place. Trim the edges to match.

Make Several And Use Them To Create
A Festive Seder Atmosphere!!!

ELIJAH'S CUP WALL HANGING

You Will Need:
1 piece white cardboard - 9" x 12"   colored yarn
colored crayons   hole puncher
popsicle stick or paper clip   several black crayons

STEP 1 - Color the entire piece of tagboard with colored crayons. Make no specific design and keep it very colorful. Press hard.

STEP 2 - Color over your colored design with the black crayons. Make sure to cover up your entire design.

STEP 3 - Use the popsicle stick or stretched out paper clip to scratch out a large wine cup (See Jewish Symbol Patterns pages 137-144) in the middle of the cardboard.

STEP 4 - Scratch more decorations around the wine cup and even inside of it.

STEP 5 - Punch a hole at the top for hanging and several on the bottom and sides of your picture as well.

STEP 6 - Cut several pieces of yarn and tie them to the holes for fringe.

Hang On Your Door To Welcome
Elijah To Your Seder!

ELIJAH'S CUP HOLDER

You Will Need:
3 paper or plastic cups   glue
masking tape   colored yarn

STEP 1 - Take a piece of masking tape and make a ring, sticky side out.

STEP 2 - Turn a cup upside down on the table in front of you. Place the tape ring on top of the upside down cup. Place another cup right-side-up on top of the tape ring, attaching them.

STEP 3 - Pressing down slightly, take some additional tape and wrap it around the cups where they are joined.

STEP 4 - Cover your cups with glue. Take colored yarn and wrap it around the cups, covering the cups completely. Use several colors to make stripes of various sizes.

STEP 5 - When dry, place the third cup in the top of your Elijah's cup holder.

AFIKOMAN HOLDER

You Will Need
1 piece tagboard - 8 ½" x 11"
36" piece of yarn
crayons, markers and stickers   hole puncher

STEP 1 - Place the tagboard in front of you lengthwise. Fold the bottom edge up towards the top leaving about two inches from the top.

STEP 2 - Punch 6 holes on the right side, 6 on the left side, and 6 on the top.

STEP 3 - Decorate the holder as you like using crayons, markers and stickers.

STEP 4 - Tie a knot in the yarn at the left bottom corner and lace the yarn in and out following the direction of the holes.

STEP 5 - Tie a knot in the yarn at the final punch to secure it. Separate the yarn ends to make fringes.

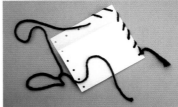

You're Ready To Hide And Find The Afikoman!

STENCIL MATZAH COVER

You Will Need:
sponges cut into small squares   paper plates
1 men's white cotton handkerchief
various colors of paint   scissors   newspaper
1 piece of tagboard or heavy drawing paper

STEP 1 - Cover your work area with newspaper.
STEP 2 - Lay out the white handkerchief on the newspaper.
STEP 3 - Pour some paint onto a paper plate. You will need a different plate
for each color you want to use.
STEP 4 - Cut out different Passover symbols (See Jewish Symbol Patterns
pages 137-144) from tagboard.

STEP 5 - Lay the cut out symbols on your
handkerchief and use a sponge to
blot paint around the symbol
shapes.
STEP 6 - Repeat this with as many symbols
or colors as you like.

When Dried, It Will Be A Beautiful Addition
To Your Seder Table!!

*GREAT IDEA! To add sparkle, use a little sparkle fabric paint
or glitter glue to accent your stencil's design.*

FROG BOUNCER

You Will Need:
3 sheets green construction paper - 9" x 12"
green yarn, about 36" long   white paper circles - 2"
black marker   glue   scissors   stapler

STEP 1 - Cut eight -1" x 12" strips from one sheet of the green colored construction paper.

STEP 2 - Fold the second sheet of green construction paper in half lengthwise and cut off the top corners of the paper making 2 triangles.

STEP 3 - On this same piece, cut a straight strip of paper off the bottom, about 2" wide. This is your frog body.

STEP 4 - Cut 4 semi circle designs, about 3" out of the third green construction paper to make your frog's feet. Cut a zigzag design along the flat end for toes.

STEP 5 - Take 2 of the green paper strips and glue one end together, forming a large strip. Take the piece on the right and fold this over to the left. Take the piece from the top and fold this down towards you. Take the piece from the left and fold it back to the right. Take the piece facing down and fold it back up to the top.

STEP 6 - Repeat this until all the paper is used. Glue the bottoms together – you have made a spring leg. Repeat this 3 more times.

STEP 7 - Glue a green "foot" to one end of each of the 4 spring legs you've made.

STEP 8 - Glue the 4 legs to the bottom of the frog body cut earlier.

STEP 9 - Glue the white circles to the top of the body and draw in pupils with black marker for the eyes.

STEP 10 - Attach the green yarn to the body by stapling it to the center and tying a knot in the top to secure it.

Now, Holding The String,
Watch Your Passover Frog Bounce His Way
Into Your Seder And Become A Happy Tradition
For Years To Come!

KARPAS PLATE

You Will Need:
1 small clear plastic cup   liquid starch
2 clear plastic plates   glue
cotton balls   glitter
blue & green tissue paper cut into 3" squares

STEP 1 - Use the cotton balls to spread a layer of liquid starch into the middle of one clear plastic plate. Place tissue paper squares over the liquid starch, covering each piece with more starch as you go. (The more tissue paper you add the deeper the colors will appear)

STEP 2 - Sprinkle some glitter over the still wet tissue paper and starch.

STEP 3 - Place some glue around the plate rim. Place the second plate on top, pressing the rims together to secure them.

STEP 4 - In the center of the top plate, glue the small clear plastic cup. This will be the salt water holder.

When Dried, You Will Have
A Beautiful And Functional Karpas Plate
To Use At Your Family Seder – Enjoy!!!

PASSOVER SEDER PILLOW

You Will Need:
feathers, sequins or glitter   stapler   glue
2 pieces of colored felt - 10" x 12"
8 sheets of paper towel   paint

STEP 1 - Decorate 2 pieces of colored felt with Passover designs (See
Jewish Symbol Patterns pages 137-144) by using feathers, sequins
or glitter and paints. Set this aside to dry.

STEP 2 - Place the 2 felt pieces together decorated sides out. Staple 3 sides
closed.

STEP 3 - Gently stuff the pillow with the paper towel sheets.

STEP 4 - Staple the final side closed.

YOM HASHOAH

YOM HASHOAH MEMORIAL LIGHT

You Will Need:
1 empty tin can   water
1 votive candle   hammer   nail

STEP 1 - Fill the tin can ¾ of the way full with water. Place the tin can in the freezer until it is completely frozen.

STEP 2 - Take the frozen tin can out of the freezer and, with a grownup's help, use a hammer and nail to carefully punch a design (See Jewish Symbol Patterns pages 137-144) into the sides of the tin can.

STEP 3 - Let the ice melt and wipe dry.

STEP 4 - Place the votive candle into the can.

On Yom Hashoah, Light Your Memorial Candle
To Remember All Of The People Who Are No Longer With Us
And All Of Our Jewish Heroes Of The Past.

YOM HASHOAH MEMORY BOX

You Will Need:
stickers   jewels
yarn   shoe box
1 sheet colored construction paper
1 large sheet of butcher paper or
other roll paper
Glue   scissors

STEP 1 - Wrap the shoe box with the butcher paper. Wrap the top separately.

STEP 2 - Cut out different symbols and shapes out of the colored
construction paper (See Jewish Symbol Patterns pages 137-144.)

STEP 3 - Decorate the shoe box and the top with the stickers, jewels, yarn
and colored construction paper cutouts.

When Your Memory Box Is Complete,
Use It To Hold Items That Help You Remember
People, Places And Things!

YOM HA'ATZMAUT

ISRAELI FLAG

You Will Need:
1 sheet white construction paper - 12" x 18"
1 sheet blue construction paper - 12" x 18"
1 sheet brown construction paper - 9" x 12"
glue or tape   scissors   blue glitter

STEP 1 - Tightly roll the brown piece of construction paper, lengthwise, to make a flag pole. Glue or tape the ends closed.

STEP 2 - Place a 2" wide strip of glue along one of the short edges of the white paper.

STEP 3 - Place the brown rolled paper on the glue end. Leave about 6" of rolled paper exposed at the bottom.

STEP 4 - Roll the white paper once around to cover the flag pole.

STEP 5 - Cut 2 triangles, about 4" each side, and 2 long strips, from the blue construction paper. Cut out the center of each triangle.

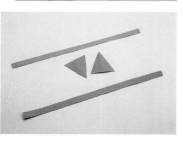

STEP 6 - To make the Star of David, glue one triangle in the middle of the white construction paper and another triangle on top of the first one, pointed in the opposite direction.

STEP 7 - Glue 1 long strip about an inch from the top of the white construction paper and the other an inch from the bottom. Drizzle glue over the blue pieces and sprinkle with blue glitter.

ISRAELI ART

You Will Need:
colored chalk   glue   table salt
several small bowls   newspaper
1 sheet tagboard - 9" x 12" or a thick paper plate

STEP 1 - Spread newspaper over work area.

STEP 2 - Pour some salt into a mixing bowl and color the salt with a piece of colored chalk. This will take a little while.

STEP 3 - Repeat the entire process with other colored chalk.

STEP 4 - Draw a Jewish design on a sheet of tagboard or paper plate (See Jewish Symbol Patterns pages 137-144).

STEP 5 - Put a coating of glue over an area of your design.

STEP 6 - Slowly pour whichever color of salt you want over the glued area. Pat it down gently and pour the extra salt off onto the newspaper.

STEP 7 - Repeat using as many different colors as you like.

YOM HA'ATZMAUT BANNER

You Will Need:
white roll paper - 24" x 36"   markers or crayons
1 sheet colored construction paper   glue
hole puncher   scissors   string for hanging

STEP 1 - Cut out holiday symbols (See Jewish Symbol Patterns pages 137-144) from the colored construction paper. Use the crayons or markers to decorate the symbols.

STEP 2 - Glue the cutout symbols onto the white roll paper.

STEP 3 - Write a happy birthday message to the State of Israel.

STEP 4 - Punch 4 holes in the banner, one hole in each corner. Tie strings to the holes and hang your banner where everyone can share in the celebration!

Yom Ha'Atzmaut Is A Great Time To Show Your Pride In The State Of Israel. Nothing Says It Better Than A Bright Banner To Wish Israel A Happy Birthday!

LAG B'OMER

ARROW AND QUIVER SUNCATCHER

You Will Need:
1 sheet black construction paper   scissors
2 pieces of clear contact paper - 5" x 7"
yarn or ribbon for hanging   hole puncher
colored tissue paper cut into small squares

STEP 1 - Cut arrow and quiver (arrow holder) silhouettes from the black construction paper. Cone shapes can be used to represent the quivers.

STEP 2 - Place your silhouettes as you like on the contact paper, sticky side up.

STEP 3 - Place colored tissue paper around silhouettes to add color.

STEP 4 - Place second sheet of clear contact paper on top, sticky side down, to seal it.

STEP 5 - Punch a hole and string a ribbon at the top for hanging.

To Add Additional Interest, Punch A Border Of Holes All The Way Around Your Suncatcher. Lace Around The Outside Using Yarn Or Ribbon.
You Can Also Create A Border By Tying Yarn Around The Outside, Creating A Fringe Effect.

GREAT IDEA! Colored cellophane can be substituted for tissue paper.

LAG B'OMER
PENCILS AND HOLDER

You Will Need:
feathers   scissors   glue
4 pencils   empty tin can
brown, red and yellow construction paper

STEP 1 - Cut the brown construction paper to fit the height and width of the tin can.

STEP 2 - Cover the tin can with glue and roll the brown construction paper on, to cover the can.

STEP 3 - Cut 4 triangles out of the yellow construction paper and 4 triangles out of the red construction paper. Make sure the triangles are more or less the same size and big enough to fit on the end of the pencil.

STEP 4 - Glue the feathers to the red triangles along the edges. Glue 2 feathered triangles back-to-back onto the eraser end of 2 pencils.

STEP 5 - Glue yellow arrowhead pairs onto the eraser ends of the remaining 2 pencils.

Place The Pencil Arrows In The Tin Can Quiver
And Have A Great Lag B'Omer Centerpiece
Or Desk Set That Can Be Used!

LAG B'OMER RAINBOW FLYER

You Will Need:
red orange, yellow, green, blue
and purple crepe paper cut
into 24" long strips
crayons or markers
glitter   glue   stickers
2 paper plates
scissors   stapler or glue
hole puncher
string for hanging

STEP 1 - Cut out the center of both paper plates.

STEP 2 - Turn the plates upside down and decorate them with flower and plant designs.

STEP 3 - Attach the crepe paper strips along the outer edge of the inside of one of the decorated plates using staples or glue.

STEP 4 - Attach the 2 plates together using staples or glue. (Make sure the decorated sides are facing out and the crepe paper strips are hanging down)

STEP 5 - Punch a hole at the top of the rainbow flyer and tie on a string for hanging.

Hang Your Finished Lag B'Omer Rainbow Flyer In Front Of An Open Window And Watch It Dance In The Breeze.

118

SHAVUOT

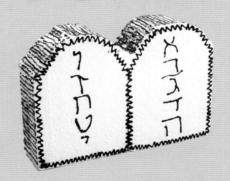

TEN COMMANDMENTS FOLDOUT

You Will Need:
1 sheet colored construction paper - 12" x 18"
1 sheet white paper - 9" x 12"   glue
markers, crayons or paints   scissors

STEP 1 - Fold the colored sheet of paper in half, widthwise. Open the paper up and fold each of the side edges into the center so that they meet at the fold line.

STEP 2 - Fold the paper again along the center fold. Cut a tablet shape from the paper by cutting a curved top.

STEP 3 - Open folded paper and you should see four curved top sections.

STEP 4 - Take the two outer sections and fold these in toward the center. Decorate as you like.

STEP 5 - Fold the white paper, widthwise, and cut a tablet shaped curve in the top.

STEP 6 - Write your own personal commandments for living or the Ten Commandments as we know them.

Display Your Commandments To Remind Yourself
Of The Laws Of The Jewish People.

POPPY IN A POT

You Will Need:
clay or plastic pot 3"-4" diameter
green yarn   popsicle stick   potting moss
flower arranging foam block   glue
colored tissue paper   black tissue paper

STEP 1 - Cover the center ⅓ of the popsicle stick with glue.

STEP 2 - Wrap the green yarn around the glue completely.

STEP 3 - Cut the colored tissue paper into 4"x4" squares.

STEP 4 - Place a square of colored tissue paper on a table or work surface. Place your index finger into the center of the square tissue paper and wrap the tissue around your finger.

STEP 5 - Dip your wrapped finger into glue and press down on one end of the popsicle stick, then remove your finger from the tissue paper.

STEP 6 - Wrap a different color of tissue paper around your finger and dip into glue. Press your tissued finger into the flower. The more tissue paper you add, the bigger your flower will become.

STEP 7 - Tear a small piece of black tissue paper and roll it into a ball. Then glue it into the center of your flower.

STEP 8 - Place some flower arranging foam into the pot.

STEP 9 - Spread glue on top of the foam and paste the potting moss on.

STEP 10 - Press the clean end of the popsicle stick firmly into the foam.

No Need To Water!
Beautiful!!

122

FLOWER HAT

You Will Need:
1 strip tagboard - 3" x 24"
6 strips tagboard - 3" x 12"
colored tissue paper cut into 3" squares
glue   stapler   scissors

STEP 1 - Measure the tagboard strip to fit around your head. Staple the ends together. This is the base of your hat.

STEP 2 - Staple the 6 strips of tagboard onto the base of your hat, from one side to the opposite, overlapping one another.

STEP 3 - Place a square of colored tissue paper on the table or work surface. Place your index finger in the center of the square tissue paper and wrap the tissue around your finger.

STEP 4 - Dip your wrapped finger into glue and paste the tissue onto one of the strips of tag board.

STEP 5 - Repeat steps 2 and 3 and add these colorful flowers to all 6 construction paper strips.

Put On Your Flower Hat And Enjoy The Season!!

Holiday Suggestion: for an added touch spray your hat lightly with your favorite floral perfume – beautiful.

TEN COMMANDMENTS TABLET SCULPTURE

You Will Need:
2 pieces of styrofoam (floral foam) - 2" thick
plastic butter knife   glue
black, gold or silver fabric paint

STEP 1 - Use the knife to cut the top of each foam piece into a curve.
STEP 2 - Glue the 2 foam pieces together side by side to look like 2 tablets.
STEP 3 - Paint an outline along the outside edges of the 2 tablets. You can write the letters of the Aleph Bet on the front of the tablets or simply horizontal lines to look like writing.

Your Tablet Sculpture Will Look Great.... Enjoy!

GREAT IDEA! Pieces of black yarn can be glued in place instead of using the fabric paint.

SHABBAT

STENCIL CHALLAH COVER

You Will Need:
1 men's white cotton handkerchief   scissors
various colors of paint   newspapers
1 piece tagboard   paper plates   sponges

STEP 1 - Cover your work area with newspaper to protect your work surface.

STEP 2 - Spread out the white cotton handkerchief on top of the newspapers.

STEP 3 - Cut the sponges into small squares.

STEP 4 - To make stencil shapes, cut out different Shabbat symbols, about 3" high (see Jewish Symbol Patterns pages 137-144), from the tagboard.

STEP 5 - Pour some paint onto a paper plate. You will need a different plate for each color you want to use.

STEP 6 - Place a stencil on the handkerchief.

STEP 7 - Dip the sponge square into one of the colors of paint. Blot the paint to fill the cutout. Then carefully lift off the stencil.

STEP 8 - Repeat step 7 with the different Shabbat symbols and colors of paint.

Let Your Project Dry Completely.
You're Now Ready To Enjoy Your
Hand-Crafted Challah Cover!

GREAT IDEA! Use glitter fabric paint or glitter glue to accent your stencils and add a little sparkle.

CLAY COIL CANDLE HOLDERS

You Will Need:

self-hardening clay   2 Shabbat candles
assorted colors of paint   glitter

STEP 1 - Knead a handful of self-hardening clay until it is easy to work with.

STEP 2 - Take some of the clay and form it into 2 balls, about the size of a marble.

STEP 3 - Flatten the clay balls into a disc shape a little larger than the bottom of the Shabbat candle.

STEP 4 - Place one of the Shabbat candles in the middle of one of the clay discs.

STEP 5 - Take some more clay and roll it into 2 more balls, about the size of golf balls. Use a squeezing and rolling motion to make snakes out of the balls.

STEP 6 - Place one end of the clay snake onto the clay disc and pressing them together. Now wrap the snake around the candle until you reach the end of the snake. Carefully remove the candle.

STEP 7 - Repeat step 6 with the second clay disc.

STEP 8 - Dip your fingers in water and gently smooth the water over the coils of clay, securing the pieces together.

Allow Several Days For The Clay Coil Candle Holders
To Dry Completely.
When Dry, You Can Decorate As You Like.

HAVDALLAH SPICE BOX

You Will Need:
1 empty baby-food jar & lid   liquid starch
colored tissue paper, cut into squares   cotton balls
glitter or jewels   hammer   paint
cinnamon sticks, cloves, and potpourri
newspapers   nail

STEP 1 - Cover your work area with newspapers.

STEP 2 - Remove the lid from the jar. Turn the empty jar upside down.

STEP 3 - Use the cotton balls to spread a layer of liquid starch over the jar.

STEP 4 - Place tissue paper squares on the jar. Cover jar with another layer of liquid starch. Set this aside to dry.

STEP 5 - With the help of an adult, use the hammer and nail to punch several holes into the top of the baby food lid.

STEP 6 - Paint the baby food lid to match the tissue colors used on the jar. Set this aside to dry.

STEP 7 - When both items are dry, decorate the baby food jar and lid by gluing on glitter or gemstones. Be sure not to cover the holes in the baby food lid.

STEP 8 - Place some cinnamon, cloves and scented potpourri in the jar and close with the lid.

Now, It's Ready For Your Havdallah Service To Add Some Spice To Your Week To Come!

FELT KIPPAH

You Will Need:
1 sheet felt - 9" x 12"   scissors
1 plate - 9"   pencil
markers   glue   stapler
fabric paints or glitter

STEP 1 - Place the plate on top of the sheet of felt. Trace around the plate with your pencil.

STEP 2 - Cut out the circle shape.

STEP 3 - Cut on an angle several 2" slits going up along the edge of the circle.

STEP 4 - Slightly overlap the cut slits and secure them with staples.

STEP 5 - Repeat step 4 all around the circle.

STEP 6 - Decorate the felt kippah with markers, fabric paints or glitter.

Now You Have Your Very Own,
Personally Created Kippah!!!

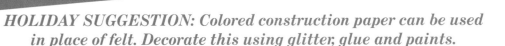

HOLIDAY SUGGESTION: Colored construction paper can be used in place of felt. Decorate this using glitter, glue and paints.

BEESWAX CANDLES

You Will Need:
5 sheets colored beeswax
4" white Shabbat candles
scissors

STEP 1 - Cut one beeswax sheet into strips.

STEP 2 - Cut four 3" wide pieces of beeswax, one for each candle.

STEP 3 - Wrap each white Shabbat candle with a piece of beeswax, pressing it while covering the candle. Be sure to leave about an inch at the bottom of each candle uncovered so that it will fit into a candle holder.

STEP 4 - Decorate your beeswax candles with the cutout beeswax strips, by gently pressing them against the candle.

Once You're Candle Is Decorated It Can Be Used As A Wonderful, Colorful Part Of Your Next Shabbat Celebration!

JEWISH SYMBOL PATTERNS FOR TRACING

138

139

141

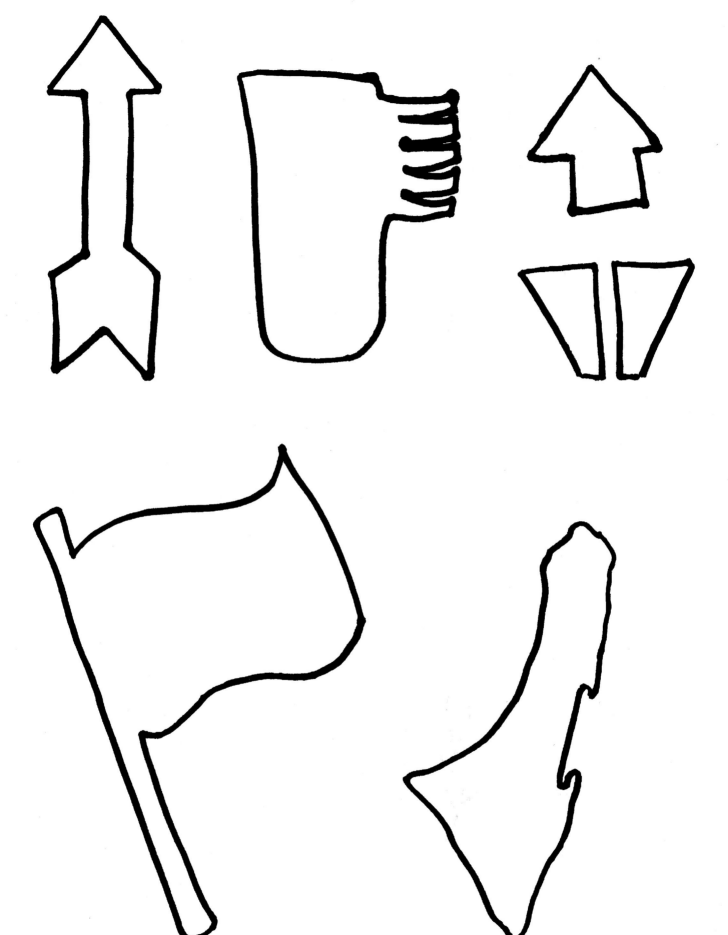

143